THE CONOCO-ANN HORNAK CHILDREN'S PICTURE BOOK COLLECTION

Honoring 39 years of service to Houston Public Library by Assistant Director Ann Hornak. This collection specially salutes Miss Hornak's outstanding contributions to children's library services. Her innovative programs and selfless dedication will continue to introduce children of all ages to the exciting world of literature.

houston Public libraries

conoco
a DuPont company

HAVE YOU
EVER WISHED
YOU WERE
SOMETHING
ELSE?

HAVE YOU EVER WISHED YOU WERE SOMETHING ELSE?

CHILDRENS PRESS, CHICAGO

By Richard Armour

Illustrated by Scott Gustafson

Dedicated to Shelley, Alex, Michael, and Gregory

Library of Congress Cataloging in Publication Data

Armour, Richard Willard, 1906–
   Have you ever wished you were something else?

   Summary: A collection of poems dealing with the good and bad things about being an ant, eagle, fish, elephant, or other creature.
   1. Animals—Juvenile poetry.   2. Children's poetry, American. [1. Animals—Poetry.
2. American poetry]   I. Gustafson, Scott, ill.
II. Title.
PS3501.R55H3   811'.52   81-17102
ISBN 0-516-03475-8   AACR2

Copyright © 1983 by Regensteiner Publishing Enterprises, Inc.
All rights reserved. Published simultaneously in Canada.
Printed in the United States of America.
   2 3 4 5 6 7 8 9 10 R 92 91 90 89 88 87 86 85 84

Table of Contents

AN ANT.....6

AN EAGLE.....8

A FISH.....10

AN ELEPHANT.....13

A RABBIT.....16

A BEAR.....19

A MONKEY.....22

A BEAVER.....24

A WHALE.....26

A GIRAFFE.....29

A PORCUPINE.....32

A FOX.....34

A CLAM.....36

A LION.....38

A HIPPOPOTAMUS.....42

A SPIDER.....44

AN ANT

I wish I were a tiny ant
To slip through cracks where others can't
And crawl up walls and cross a ledge
And peer unfrightened past the edge
And eat the sweets that others bought
And hurry out again uncaught.
I'd like to live down in the ground
Where, with my friends, I'd not be found
And made to brush my teeth and hair
And told what clothes I had to wear.

But come to think of it, I'm glad
I'm not an ant. It would be bad
To carry loads of heavy stuff
As big as I, where walking's rough.
And if some day someone should put
On little me his giant foot,
I'd have no voice, no way of knowing,
Nor time to shout, "Look where you're going!"
Oh, I'd be squashed and, I insist,
Still worse than that, I'd not be missed.

AN EAGLE

I wish I were an eagle soaring.
My life would never once be boring.
I'd fly on mighty wings through skies
And look around with piercing eyes
And build my nest in tallest tree
Or on a cliff. What view I'd see!
Because of large, strong bill and claws
I'd never have the slightest cause
To fear a snake or anything,
But if I did, I'd just take wing.

I'm glad I'm not an eagle really,
Despite those wings, those eyes so steely.
It would be lonely way up there
So far from earth in upper air,
And in a cliffside nest I'd frown,
For it would scare me to look down.
I envy not the eagle's life
Up in his nest with children, wife . . .
No roof, no furniture, no heat,
And mostly thinking, "What's to eat?"

A FISH

I wish I were, oh how I wish

I were a swiftly swimming fish.

Without a lesson, I'd start out

And gracefully I'd swim about.

I would not tire, my stroke so strong

I'd swim and swim the whole day long,

And if I swallowed water—well,

I wouldn't cough, no one could tell.

Imagine swimming every day,

Not just vacations. What a way!

AN ELEPHANT

An elephant appeals to me.
An elephant I'd like to be.
It would be nice to be so large
And strong that I would be in charge,
With gleaming tusks and skin so thick
You couldn't scratch me with a stick.
I'd love to have a trunk, with charm,
A combination nose and arm,
And pick up peanuts north and south
And neatly drop them in my mouth.

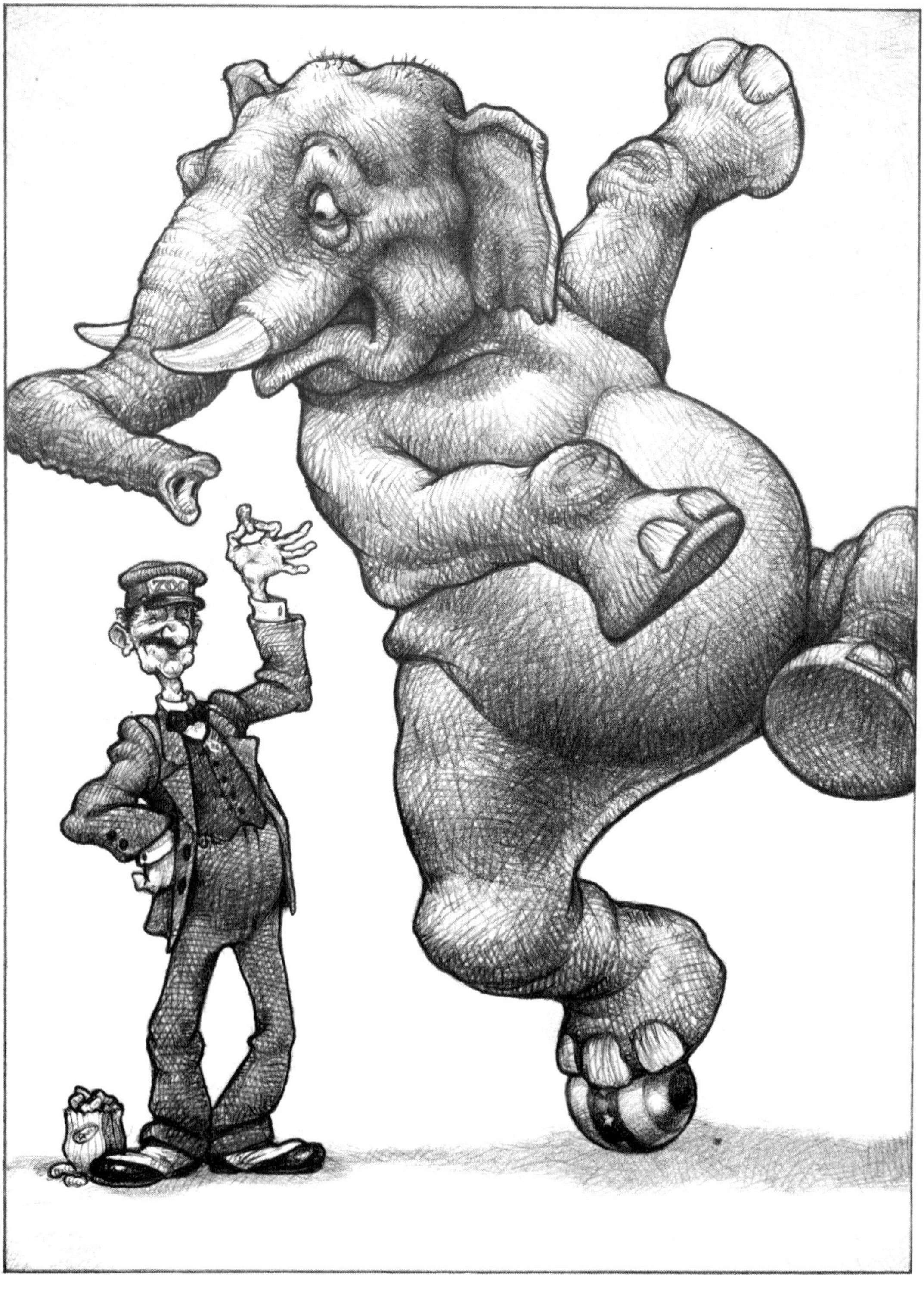

The more I think of it, the less
An elephant's for me, I guess.
I wouldn't want such big flat feet,
I'd never get enough to eat,
I wouldn't like my ears so floppy,
That plodding walk I'd hate to copy,
My skin, though thick, would be too rough,
And if all that is not enough
I'd hate to wind up in a zoo
And be taught tricks I'd *have* to do.

A RABBIT

A rabbit is among the creatures
That I find has attractive features.
I'd like to have such fur, so soft
That I'd be cuddled very oft.
If I had rabbit legs I'd bound
And leap and really cover ground.
I'd also give more than a penny
For ears that stick up like antennae
And listen to what's said of me
And have a hole to which to flee.

I'm glad that I'm not rabbit-faced
With nose that twitches, being chased
By foxes, dogs, and men with guns.
A fleeing rabbit runs and runs,
His heart a-flutter, full of fear,
His hole more likely far than near.
A rabbit's life is not so much
If part of it's spent in a hutch,
Or, since a rabbit's very yummy,
In some old sharp-toothed fox's tummy.

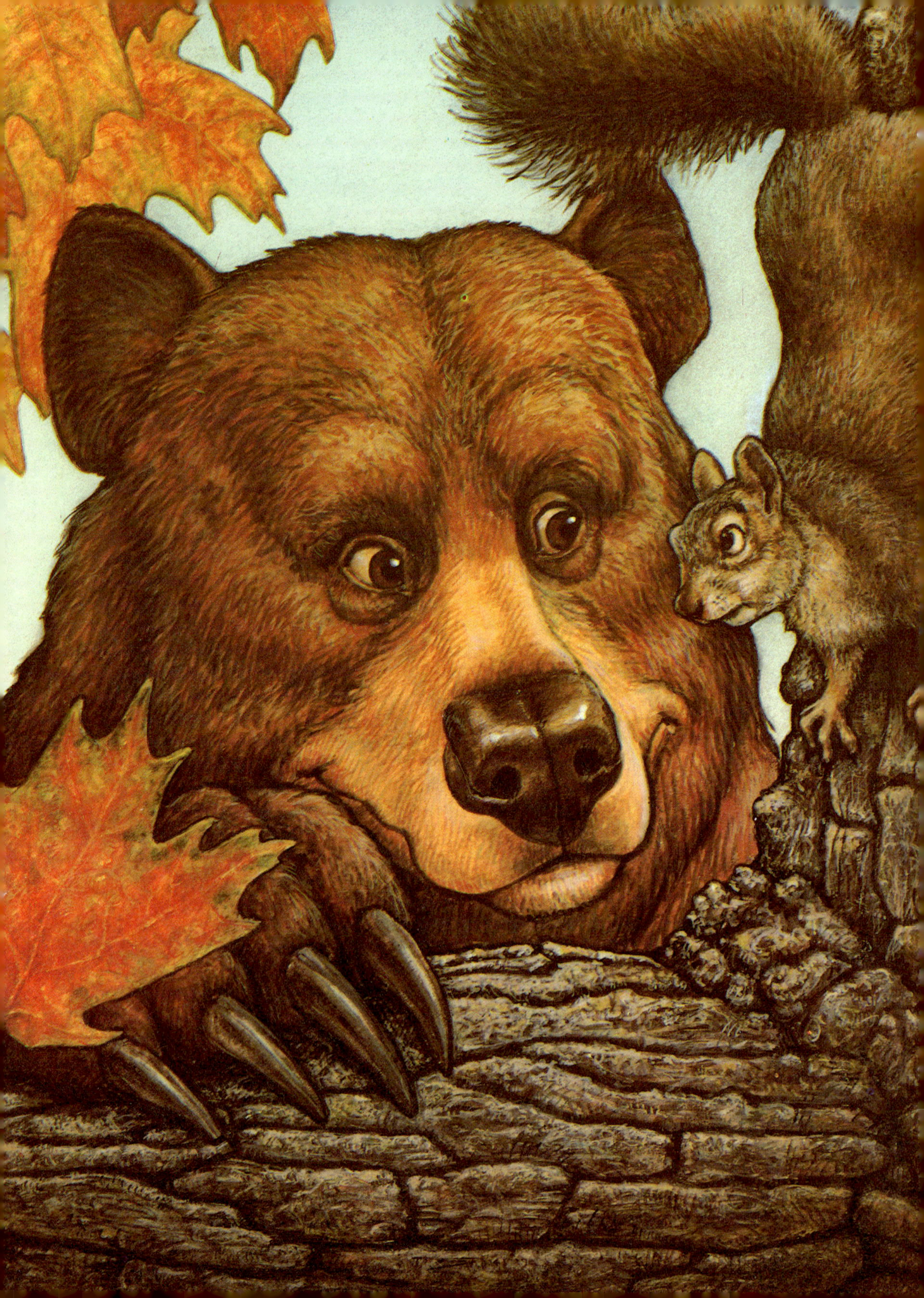

A BEAR

I wish I were a great big bear,
Some ten feet long, with shaggy hair
And pointed toenails, never clipped,
With which the trunks of trees are gripped.
A help in climbing, clawing, tightening,
They, plus those teeth, are also frightening.
Were I a bear, I wouldn't fight you,
I wouldn't claw you, wouldn't bite you,
But if I somehow couldn't bear you
I'll bet that I could really scare you.

I'm glad I'm not a bear for reasons
That mostly have to do with seasons.
In winter, I'd like hair, a lot;
In summer, though, I'd be too hot.
All winter long I'd hibernate,
Stay in my cave in sleepy state. . . .
Eight hours at night, or maybe ten,
Should be enough, in cave or pen,
But sleep so long, not run or climb?
I'd find it quite a waste of time.

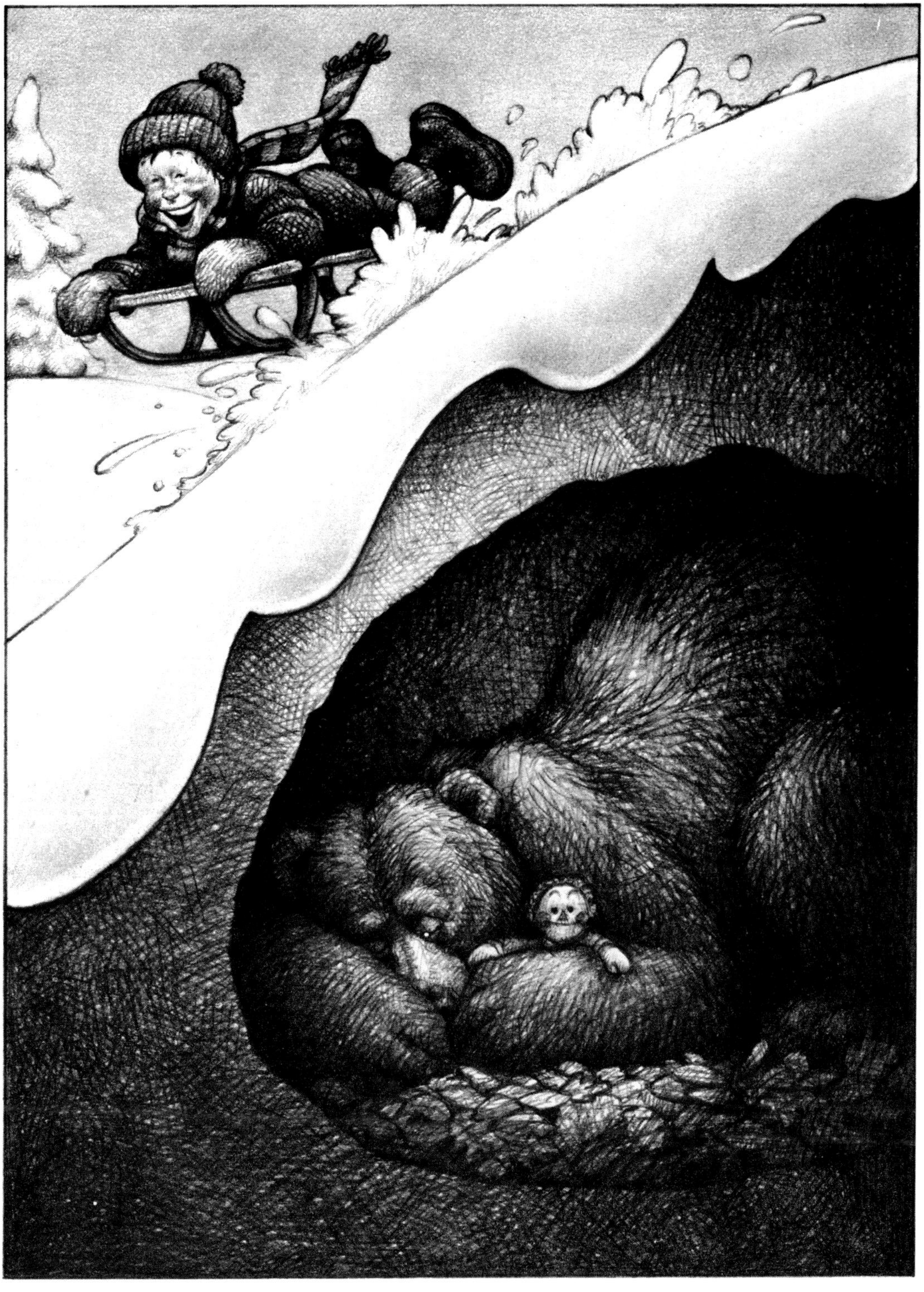

A MONKEY

A monkey's life I think I'd like,

A monkey maybe known as Mike.

From branch to branch I'd gaily swing,

Fly through the trees as if on wing.

That tail would be what I'd find grand:

I'd use it like an extra hand

And grab a branch, not even grope,

And dangle from it like a rope.

All day I'd play, eat a banana,

And have a girlfriend, name of Anna.

I'm not so sure I'd find a breeze
A monkey's life, because of fleas
On me and others always sticking
And keeping us forever picking.
Besides, if I should choose to sit,
What of that tail, what do with it?
For hanging, holding after leaping,
A tail would be quite nice for keeping,
But sitting, to the side or under?
Where put the thing? That's what I'd wonder.

A BEAVER

A beaver I could be, with joy,
To build, however, not destroy.
I'd like, with beaver's teeth and jaw,
Right through a great big tree to gnaw.
And then I'd take the logs I'd clear
And, architect and engineer,
I'd build a dam to hold back waters
And build a house that beats an otter's.
Were I a beaver—smart, hard-working—
Forgive me for my proudly smirking.

It's hard to find such an achiever
As is the always busy beaver,
And yet with all that zeal and zest
I'd want a day or two of rest.
My teeth would tire, so would my jaw;
I'd like a chisel and a saw.
Work is all right, in fact it's great,
That's why the beaver high I rate.
I'd want some rest, though, want some play,
Not work each minute of the day.

A WHALE

I often wish I were a whale,

A sort of ship without a sail.

With mighty flukes I'd swim so fast

That fish and boats would both be passed.

I'd dive down deep, then up and spout

And with my whale friends play about.

In summer I'd swim north for cooling;

In winter I'd swim south, no fooling.

Or the reverse, this navigator,

If living south of the Equator.

I'm glad I'm not a whale, though, when
I think of mean old whaling men
Who'd track me down on whaling ships
With harpoon guns upon their tips.
They, whom I'd done no slightest harm,
Well know my blubber keeps me warm
And that I've lots of whalebone growth,
And they have uses for them both.
And so, in search of bone and oil,
My lovely life at sea they'd spoil.

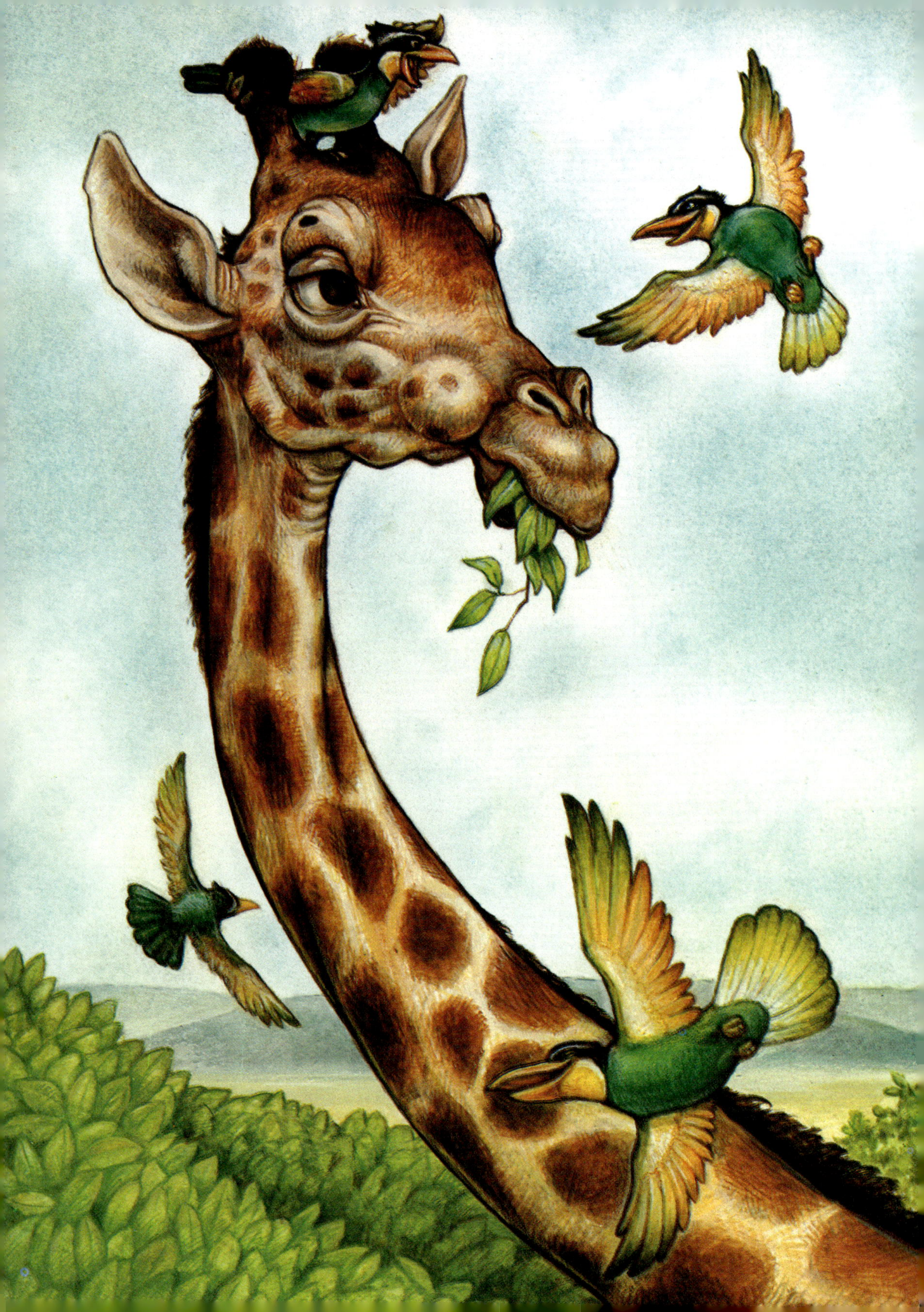

A GIRAFFE

Sometimes I wish—and please don't laugh—
I were a large, long-necked giraffe.
Eighteen feet high, what scenes I'd scan,
Three times as tall as is a man.
With such a neck, so nicely made,
I'd miss no sights at a parade,
And I could eat a fig or peach
That otherwise I couldn't reach.
If danger threatened, I of course
Could gallop faster than a horse.

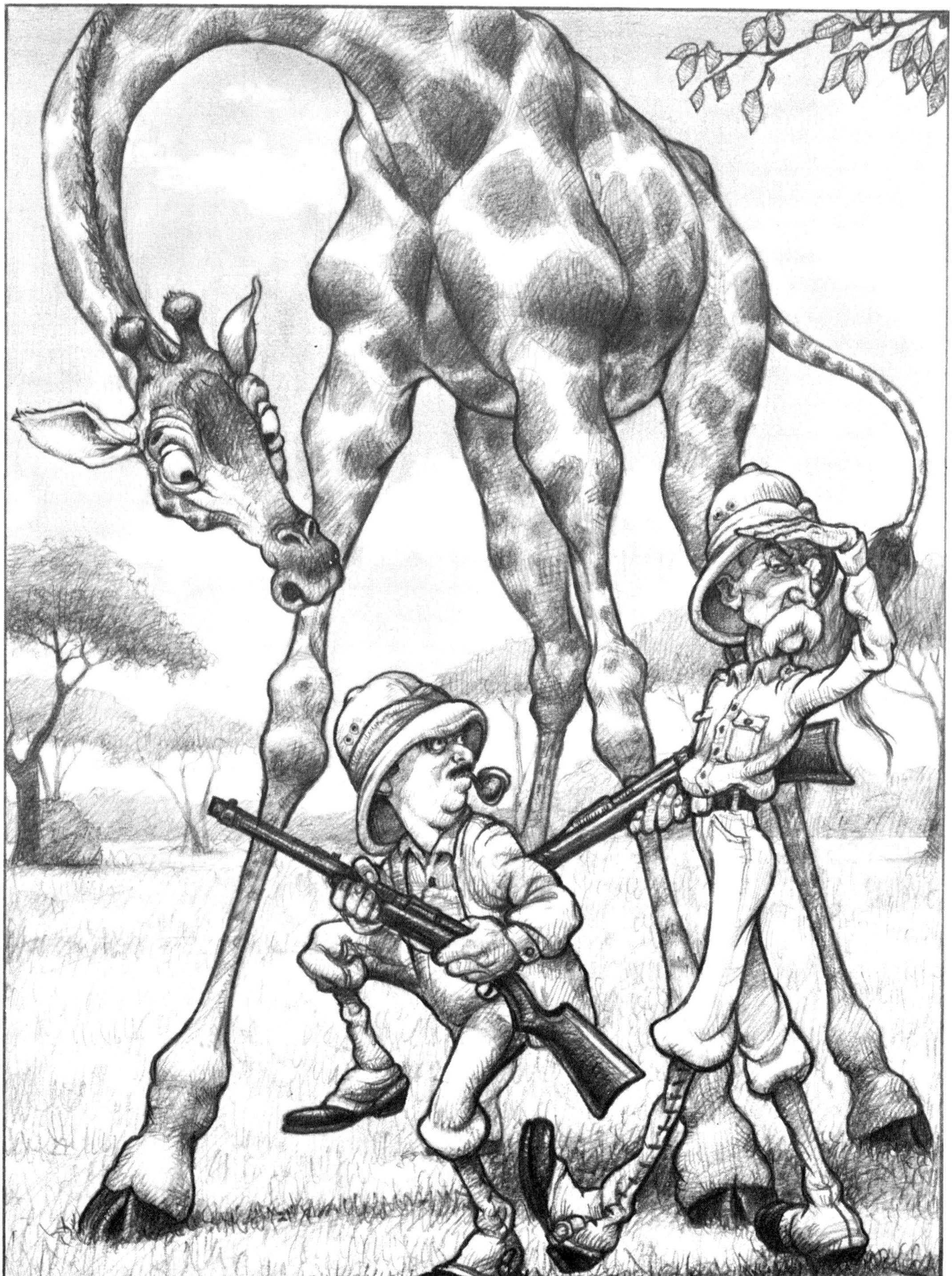

I'm glad, though, a giraffe I'm not
And living where it's always hot,
With spotted hide of white and brown
That helps the hunters hunt me down.
I'd rather have a skin like mine;
My furless skin with me is fine,
For it's no good, no good at all,
To decorate a floor or wall.
And best, when I've a throat that's sore
It's long enough, I'd want no more.

A PORCUPINE

I wish I were a porcupine
With quills that stuck out from my spine
And also covered all my tail,
A tail that I could fiercely flail.
I could not, really, shoot a quill,
But my attacker'd get his fill
If he should grab me. I would win
When quills like arrows pierced his skin.
I might be stupid, might be slow,
But I'd be left alone, I know.

A porcupine, as I have said,
Is not so brainy in the head,
And I would hate to be a beast
That wasn't slightly smart at least.
I might have quills for self-defense,
But I would also like some sense.
What good if I were safe from danger,
Yet thought by most an oddish stranger
That gnaws the bark, can kill a tree,
But can't do tricks or count to three.

A FOX

A fox is very smart at hiding
When after it someone is riding.
A fox is also good at running,
But what I envy is his cunning.
Yes, if a foxy fox I were,
As sly as anything in fur,
I'd not get stuck as sometimes now
When I'm less like a fox than cow.
I'd settle troubles, always win them—
Still foxier, I'd not get in them.

I'm glad, though, I am not a fox,
With no regard for doors and locks
And fences, too, and all the rest,
Who prowls at night, when sleep is best.
Were I a fox, I'd skulk with skill
And do some things that make me ill,
For instance sneak inside a pen
And creep up on a lamb or hen
And grab it by the throat and run. . . .
I really wouldn't call that fun.

A CLAM

When much too talkative I am,
I often wish I were a clam.
At most a clam emits a bubble,
And thus keeps out of lots of trouble.
It might be no exciting chum,
This clam within its shell, so mum,
But nestled in the mud or sand
It lives in peace, I understand.
I'd like its simple, carefree way,
And none to me ''Clam up!'' would say.

And yet I'm glad, I'm really glad
I'm not a clam. It would be sad
To spend my life stuck in the mud
And be considered such a dud.
I'd have one foot, for this is par,
But with it I'd not travel far,
Nor would I, quite without ambition,
Have any very special mission
Except to eat, the more the prouder,
And wind up maybe in clam chowder.

A LION

A lion, such a kingly beast,
I'd like to be a while at least.
A tiger might be fiercer still,
But I'd just like to look, not kill,
And be admired, when now and then
I'd saunter, yawning, from my den.
I'd flex my muscles, shake my mane,
And roar, and look with bored disdain.
With pride I'd tingle, even tungle,
To hear them say, "Lord of the jungle."

PANTHERA LEO

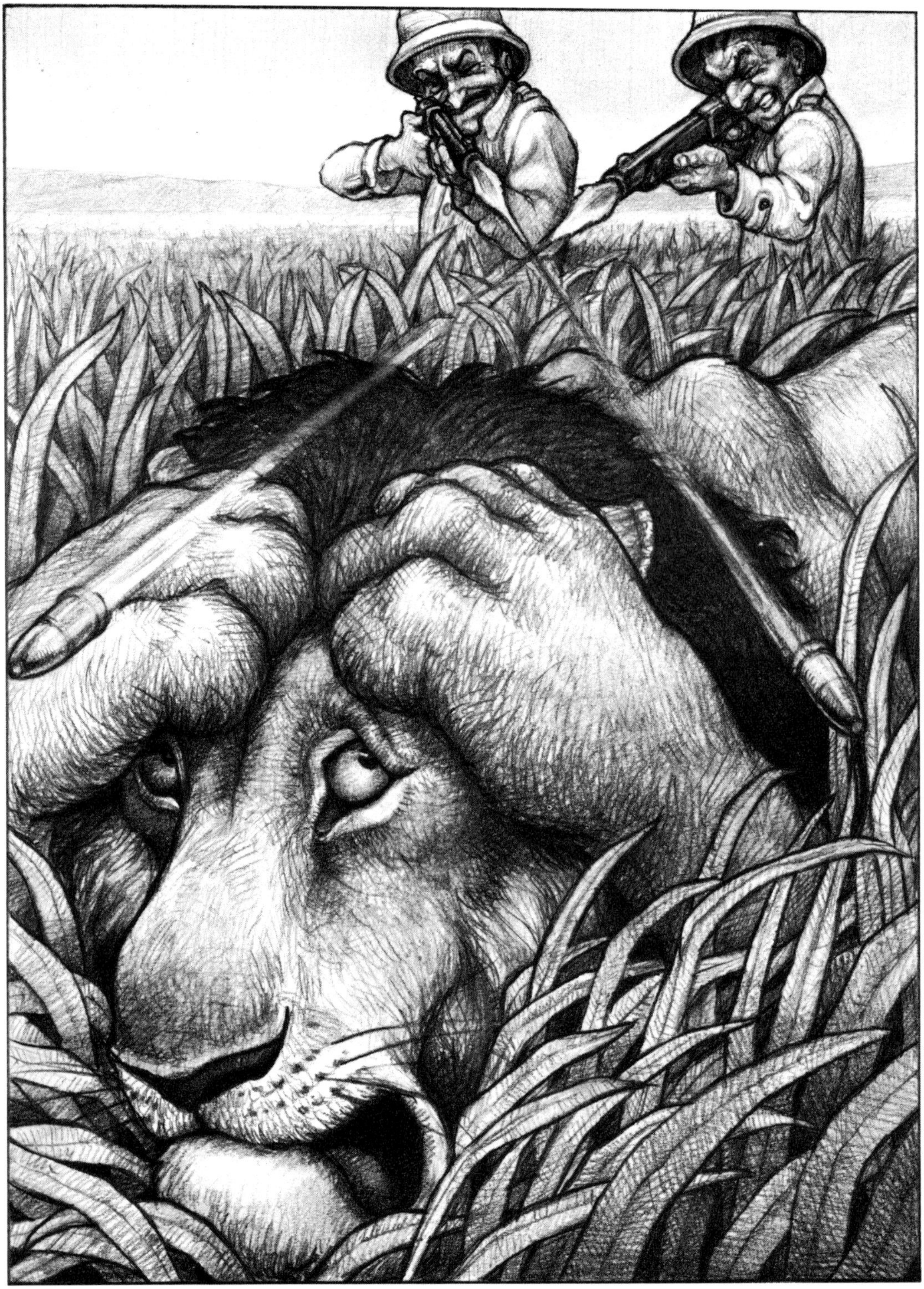

It's true that I could kill at will,

Though more from hunger than for thrill.

One blow, one bite, right in the neck

Would leave my foe a total wreck.

But I am not the least bit sorry

I'm not a lion. On safari

The hunters just for sporting trifles

And souvenirs would come with rifles

And aim and fire *(Bang! Bang!)* like this,

And I could only hope they'd miss.

A HIPPOPOTAMUS

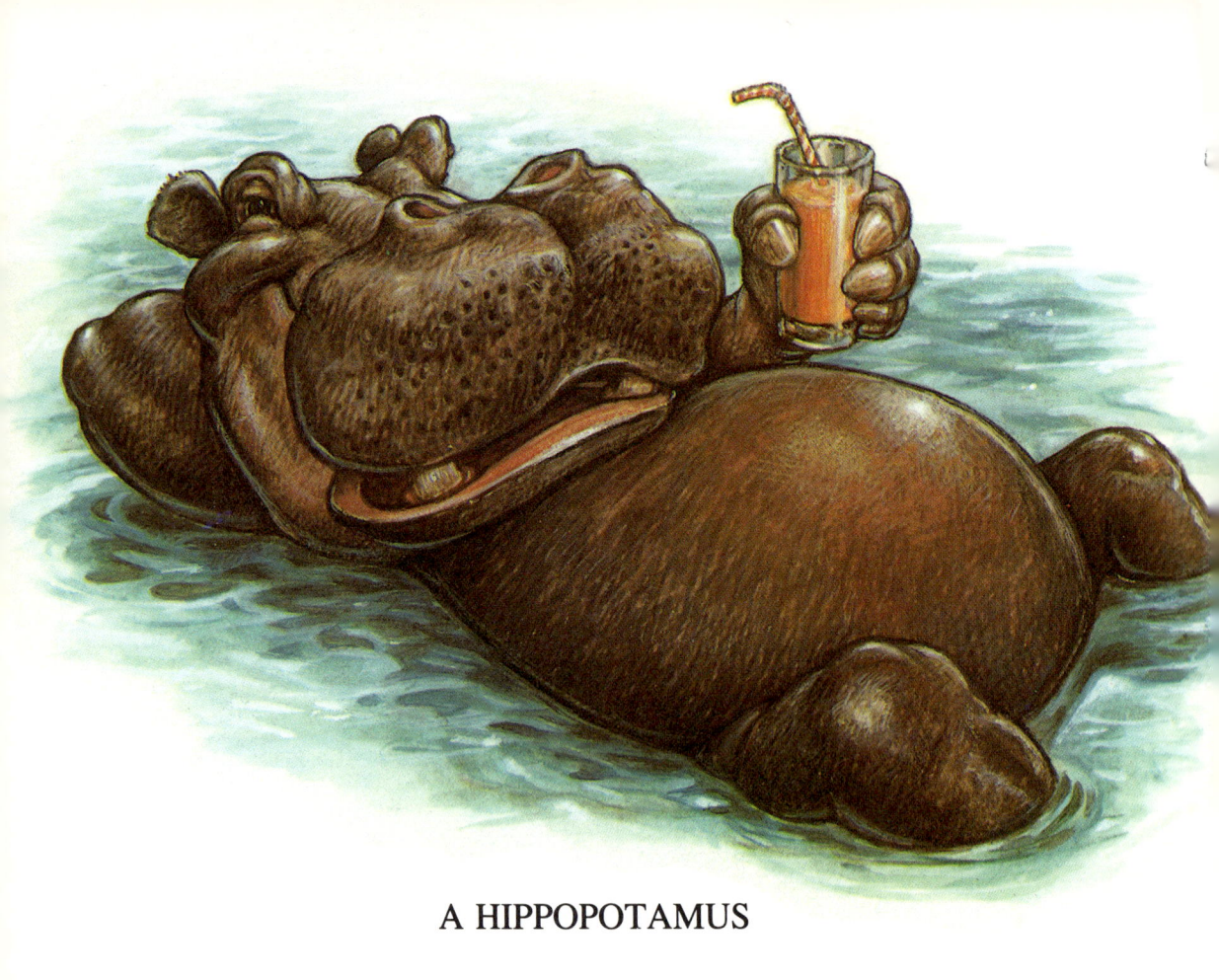

A hippopotamus would seem
To be the creature of my dream.
If I were one, I'd open wide
My mammoth mouth with look of pride,
And anyone who saw my teeth,
The ones above, the tusks beneath,
Would stay away from where I wallowed
In warmish water, or be swallowed.
Oh, thick of skin, with muscles strong,
I'd swim and sleep the whole day long.

The hippopotamus's race
Possesses such an ugly face
That it would give me quite a shiver
To see mine mirrored in a river.
My skin, too, would be an objection,
For though it gave me great protection
It's not the kind, I must confess,
That very many would caress.
From photos I have seen in books,
I simply couldn't stand my looks.

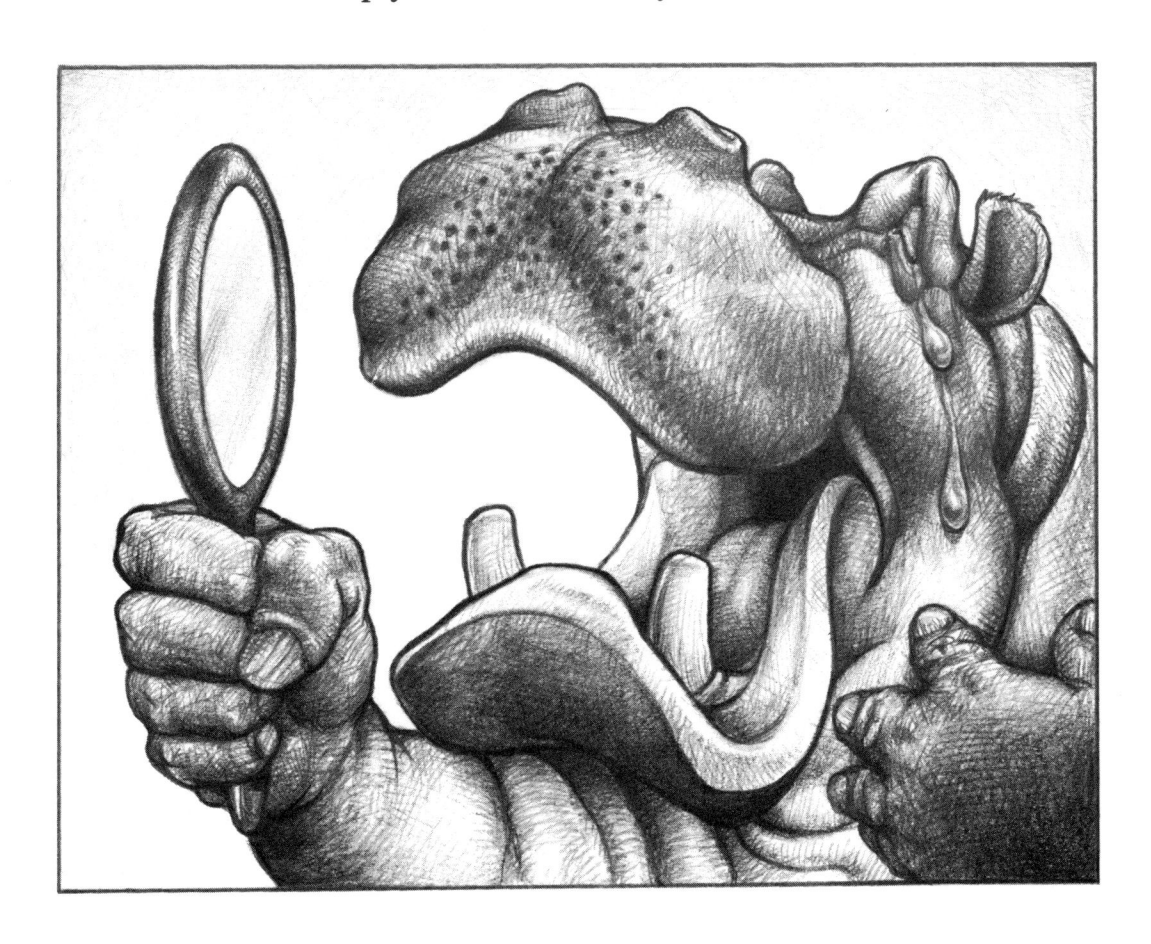

A SPIDER

I'd even like to be a spider
And spin a web that's ever wider,
With strands of silk bought from no shelf
But manufactured by myself.
Dew-damped, in morning sunshine bright
My web would be a stunning sight,
Yet it would also serve to snag
A meal of bugs. . . . I hate to brag
But with eight arms, eight eyes, I'll bet
More talent you have never met.

Although I'd catch the bugs I'd eat
And tie them up from head to feet,
And though my silky web might please,
A-flutter in a gentle breeze,
I know, alas, the angry feeling
Of those who see up on their ceiling
That web of mine—and me, awaiting
Some foolish fly. That's why I'm hating
To meet a spider's dreadful doom
When brushed down by some housewife's broom.

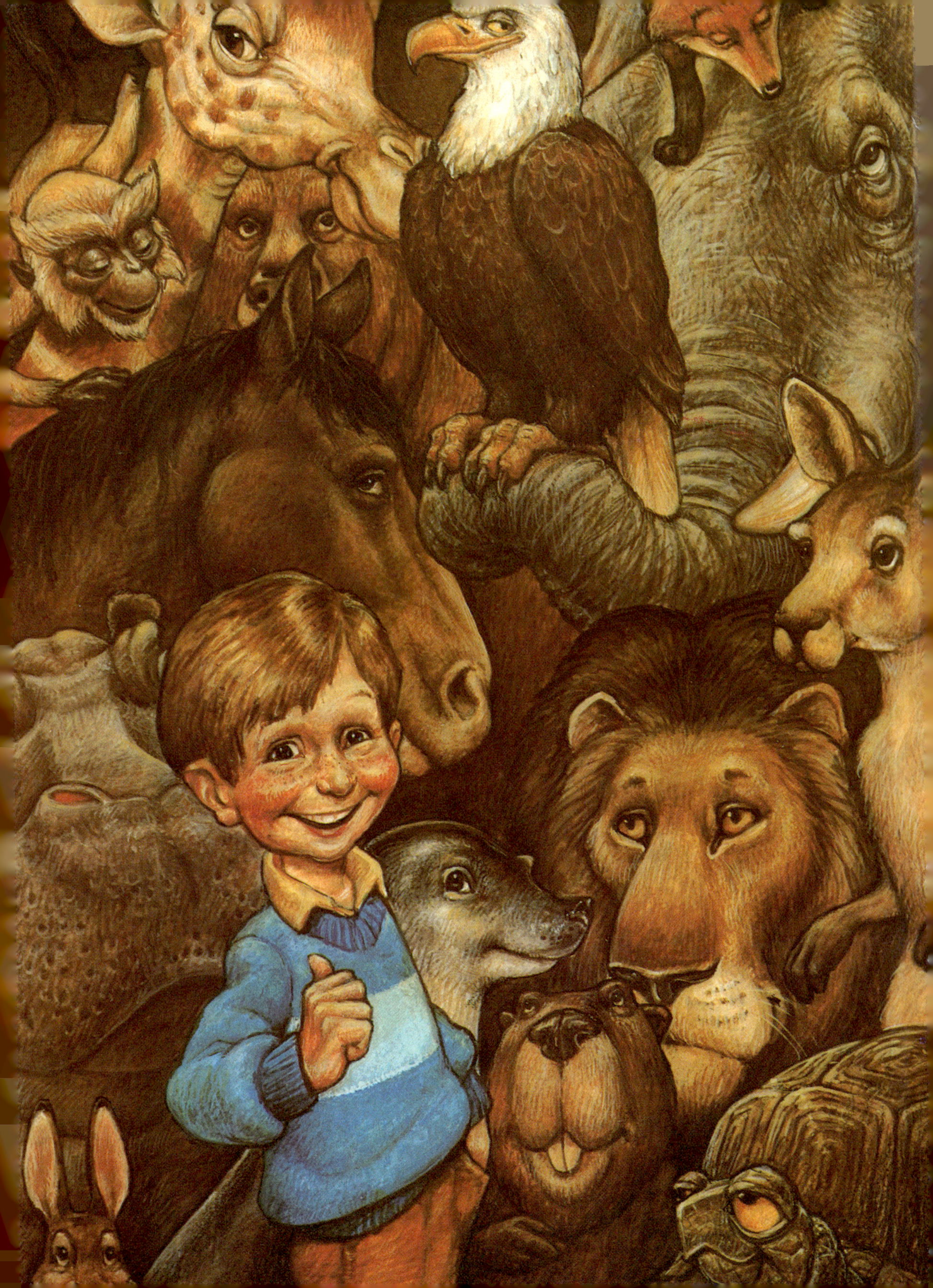

I've wished I were a kangaroo,
I've wished I were a turtle, too,
I've wished I were a dog, a cat
(There are advantages, at that),
I've wished I were a seal, of course,
I've also wished I were a horse.
I've wished I were a snake, a worm,
To feel that slither, slide, and squirm.
I've wished I were all sorts of things
With claws and shells and fur and wings.
I've wished I were a mouse, a bee,

But mostly I am glad I'm me.

ABOUT THE AUTHOR

RICHARD ARMOUR is an author who entertains and instructs readers of all ages. He says he wears two costumes, cap-and-gown and cap-and-bells. In his cap-and-gown career he is a Harvard Ph.D. who has written scholarly books of biography and literary criticism, has been a professor of English at a number of colleges and universities, and has lectured in twenty countries of Europe and Asia for the State Department. In addition to his 60 books of prose and light verse, he has written over 6,000 pieces for more than 200 magazines in the United States and England.

In his cap-and-bells career, he has written humor and satire in an incredible variety of fields, such as history (*It All Started with Columbus*, *It All Started with Marx*, etc.), literature (*Twisted Tales from Shakespeare*, *The Classics Reclassified*, etc.), sports (*Golf Is a Four-Letter Word*), medicine (*It All Started with Hippocrates* and *The Medical Muse*), teenagers (*Through Darkest Adolescence*), war and weaponry (*It All Started with Stones and Clubs*), education (*Going Around in Academic Circles*, *A Diabolical Dictionary of Education*, and *The Academic Bestiary*), librarians (*The Happy Bookers*), art (*It All Started with Nudes*), and on and on.

Of his 58 books, this is his 14th for young readers. All of them are in playful verse, and Ogden Nash described him as "a master of his craft, ingenious and witty." As in his other books, there is an amazing range of subjects, from paleontology (*A Dozen Dinosaurs*) to cetology (*Sea Full of Whales*), and from marine biology (*Strange Monsters of the Sea*) to entomology (*Insects All Around Us*). Two of his books have been school book club choices, and one has been made into a prize-winning animated film. They have been praised by *The New York Times* for their "ingenuity and imagination, fun and excitement." *Have You Ever Wished You Were Something Else?* is probably his most imaginative, and should appeal to any reader whose imagination is at its peak.

ABOUT THE ARTIST

Originally a native of Marengo, Illinois, Scott Gustafson presently lives in Chicago. He has studied at the Chicago Academy of Fine Arts and Columbia College and now does free-lance illustration for periodicals and books. When he is not working, Scott spends his time watching Bugs Bunny cartoons, viewing old movies, and, in general, just goofing around.

+S
E ARMOU

DISCARD

Armour, Richard,1906-1989.
Have you ever wished you
Central OSTKSPICBK
05/21

ARMOUR, RICHARD W.
    HAVE YOU EVER WISHED
YOU WERE SOMETHING ELSE?

R0119925704   CCR   E
                      A

NOV X X 1996

HOUSTON PUBLIC LIBRARY

CENTRAL LIBRARY
500 MCKINNEY

FEB 9 2